# Properties

# CONTENTS

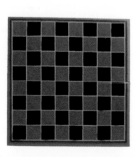

## Think About . . .

What Is Matter? ..................... 2

What Are Properties? ................. 3

What Is a Solid? .................... 5

What Is a Liquid? ................... 9

What Is a Gas? ..................... 12

## People in Science

A Geologist ....................... 14

## Did You Know?

Water Can Change ................. 15

## Glossary ........................... 16

# What Is Matter?

Look at the rocks, water, and trees. They look different. But they are alike, too. They are all made of **matter.**

# What Are Properties?

Matter makes up all things. Things have properties. **Properties** tell how something looks, smells, tastes, feels, or sounds.

### shape

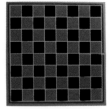

round | square

### color

red | blue

### size

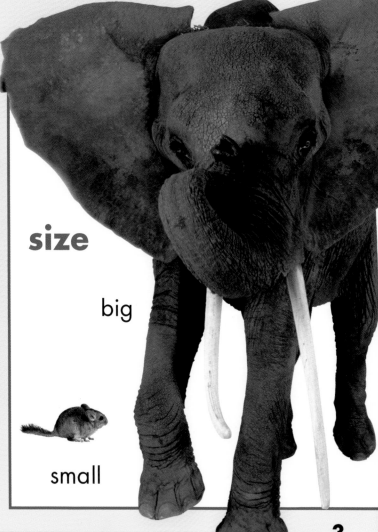

big

small

You can use properties to sort things.
Which objects are soft?
Which objects are hard?

# What Is a Solid?

A **solid** has a shape of its own.
A solid keeps its shape. A block
is a solid.

You can compare solids. We use a **balance** to compare mass. **Mass** is a property of matter.

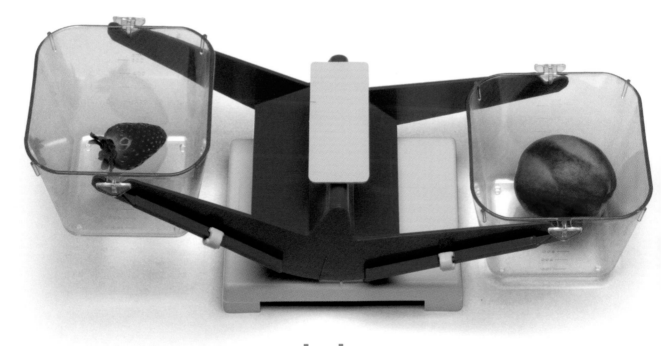

balance

You can compare solids in other ways, too. You can use your **senses.**

| texture | shape |
|---------|-------|

rough

round

smooth

square

A **magnet** pulls some objects. They are magnetic. Which objects will a magnet pull?

# What Is a Liquid?

A **liquid** does not have a shape of its own. A liquid takes the shape of its container. The shape of a liquid changes when you pour it.

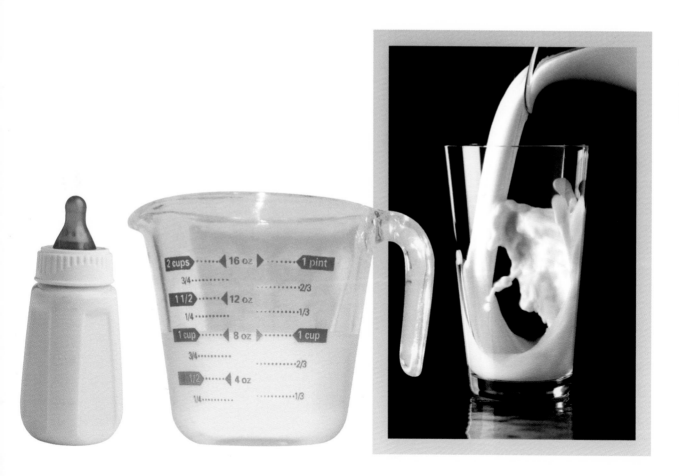

All liquids flow. Some liquids are easy to pour. Some are hard to pour.

Some things **float** on liquids.

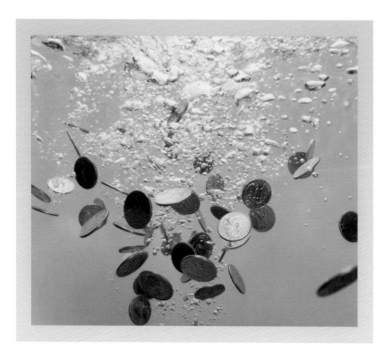

Some things **sink** in liquids.

# What Is a Gas?

A **gas** has no shape of its own.

A gas fills up all the space it can.

A balloon has air in it. Air is made of gases. We can not see most gases.

# A Geologist

A geologist studies Earth. She collects rocks. She looks at their properties. She sorts the rocks into groups. The rocks help her learn about Earth.

# Water Can Change

Water can be a **liquid.**

Water can be a **solid.**

Water can be a **gas.**

# Glossary

**balance** a tool for measuring mass

**float** to stay on top of a liquid

**gas** matter that has no shape of its own. Air is made of gases.

**liquid** matter that flows and takes the shape of its container

**magnet** a material that pulls iron or steel

**mass** how much matter is in something

**matter** anything that takes up space and has mass

**properties** how something looks, smells, tastes, feels, or sounds

**senses** what you use to find out about things; seeing, hearing, touching, tasting, smelling

**sink** to fall to the bottom of a liquid

**solid** matter that has a shape of its own